10663763

BROKER'S LIABILITY:

EMERGENCE and AVOIDANCE

(and protecting your *ASS*ets)

by: Edward N. Vink, LL.B.

Mistaya Publishing Ltd.
Calgary, Alberta

ACKNOWLEDGEMENTS

The AUTHOR wishes to thank Joan Dix for her comments and feedback that helped shape this book; Bob Stinson for his patient editing; Ted Carter, whose experience and input helped me complete the project; Ken Johnson for his encouraging comments; George Goulet for taking time out from writing his excellent book to review mine.

I must express my appreciation to the many brokers, managers and industry professionals who attended my seminars, or who, on hearing of the book, provided direction that contributed to what I hope is a useful guide.

I would also like to thank William L. Clarke, whose artistic ability was able to transform the author's primitive stickmen sketches into the illustrations that appear in this book.

The publication of this book was made possible by the support of McCaffery Goss, Barristers and Solicitors, Calgary, Alberta.

Finally, I am most grateful for the patience and encouragement of my wife, Marsha Erb, without which this book would never have been finished.

PREFACE

This book tries to achieve a balance between the "need to know" sufficient legal theory to understand origins of liability and a practical approach to avoiding liability without interfering with production.

As with all compromises, there are shortcomings. Most notably, legal theory is simplified to expedite reaching practical conclusions. For briefness the book does not refer to specific regulatory liability, for example, statutory responsibility for failing to deliver a prospectus, where obligations seem self-evident. The practical suggestions are neither exhaustive nor applicable in all situations. Notwithstanding limitations, however, if the reader develops a sensitivity to problematic situations, and through examples from the book or ideas of his own creation, reduces risk, this book will have achieved its goal.

Finally, I am aware that the industry is widely populated by women at all levels. However, I have not found any suitable way around the tiresome "his or her," or "she or he," so have kept pronouns masculine for that reason only.

CONTENTS

THE OBJECTIVES

There is no point in discussing the problem without discussing the solution. And the solution cannot become a problem of itself by interfering with productivity. The answer lies in a working understanding, a quick analysis and some efficient, practical suggestions.

"The last thing any broker needs is another reason not to do business."

That comment was made by the manager of a major brokerage firm after one of my earlier seminars on broker liability.

The point was well taken, and caused me to change the focus of my presentations. My objective was still the same - to assist the industry, and brokers in particular, in avoiding liability where possible.

However the response to my presentations indicated a second concern which needed to be addressed. That concern manifested itself in a fear that dealing with the issue of broker liability would result in an undue preoccupation with potential claims, leading to paranoia, inefficiency and loss of production.

No one was advocating a "head-in-the-sand" approach, but at the same time there was no interest in creating another problem. It would not be acceptable to discuss reduction in

1

risk of liability if it was to discourage members from pursuing their profession, boldly and without hesitation.

Accordingly, lengthy discussions of legal theory, expanded paperwork and documentation, frightening disclaimers and warnings - the stuff lawyers tend to lean on - were out of the question. Given that limitation, I had to consider whether the dual objectives of reduced risk and non-interference could be achieved.

My review of the lead cases and my experience defending brokers from claims led me to the conclusion that these seemingly contrasting objectives could indeed be attained.

Further, discussions with top producers, their managers and compliance officers convinced me that not only could we reduce risk of claims, but we could do so in a way that, rather than being offensive to the client and a drag on the producer, would be positive to both.

The solution involves three components. The first is a working understanding of what broker liability is, and how and why it arises. This is crucial, as it will allow the broker to recognize situations where exposure arises, and enable him to plan steps to reduce risk.

The second component is a quick analysis of the broker-client relationship and establishment of corresponding duties. This involves not so much a list of specific obligations but more a filter through which a broker can view his relationship with his client to determine the scope of his obligations. As we shall see, knowing when the broker's job is completed is essential, and the broker's duties will vary depending on the relationship he has with each of his clients. By using a brief, step by step "checklist" for quick analysis we can go a long way to achieving some certainty as to what the broker's obligations are, and when he has completed his task.

The third component involves some practical, efficient suggestions to reduce risk and discourage unwarranted litigation. Some surprisingly simple steps can reduce exposure, and other ideas will provide compelling evidence that there is no case to be made. The most successful cases for my broker-clients have been the ones that went away long before going to court.

Many of the suggestions are the result of consultation with members of the industry. They are by no means exhaustive. I have no doubt that industry professionals reading this, understanding the sources of liability, and seeing the kinds of things that can reduce risk, will be able to come up with a host of variations and improvements.

For me this will be a satisfying result. As a lawyer who has practised in the securities area for over 15 years I am acutely aware of the important role brokers play in the economy. I share with many of my colleagues in the legal profession (contrary, perhaps, to popular belief) a disdain for unwarranted claims. And while we may not be able to stop anyone from considering a potential lawsuit we can certainly do a few things that will dissuade the pursuit of

Now, Mr. Smith, after you've filled out the New Account Application Form, Ms. Weintraub has a few disclaimers for you to sign.

frivolous litigation.

This then is written for producers, for those who want to carry out their profession full tilt, without needless hesitation or undue cause for concern that will reduce efficiency. And it is written for office managers and compliance officers who do not want to interfere with production but also do not wish to see resources being expended defending unjust claims.

Specifically, this is not written for lawyers, as the very simplified explanations of legal theory will attest. While lawyers could debate endlessly the jurisprudence behind my conclusions (and no doubt will do so before judges) my objective is to give practical assistance, not a legal brief.

By providing a working understanding and a few suggestions, this guide should eliminate an excuse for not doing business, rather than add one.

THE GATHERING STORM

A broker's job has become more complex and responsibilities have increased. This has resulted in uncertainty about the obligations to be fulfilled. In a more litigious society, defining the broker's role is more frequently becoming the issue before the courts.

"Life," the saying goes, "used to be simpler." Regardless of how apt the observation may be on life in general, it certainly appears true for a broker.

Once upon a time a broker's job could be easily described. At law he was (and still is at the very least) an agent for the client. His role and his legal responsibility were to buy or sell stock in accordance with his client's instruction. Once that was done, his job and his exposure to liability was terminated.

There is no need to chronicle the evolution of the profession. A broker no longer simply sits back and waits for the phone to ring and orders to be placed - at least not the producer.

Even if that were his *modus operandi* the reality is that the scope of communication will go beyond just taking the order. Almost invariably the client will ask questions, seek information, discuss ideas, and a relationship will begin. With relationships come obligations.

Then, for good measure, there has evolved a responsibility for brokers to "look after" clients who may not be quite so responsible themselves. The duty to "know your client" and examine "suitability" are concepts that have evolved and are here to stay.

With the increased complexity of the position it followed that there would be increased responsibility and increased liability.

The courts began to recognize this expanded responsibility. In case after case new precedents were set and brokers and dealers were found liable for losses attributable to failures in discharging these new, greater responsibilities. If a loss occurred it became evident that the client was justified in seeing if he could recover it from his broker.

Suing brokers over losses is not a new idea. Brokers and brokerage houses have been hauled before the courts by disgruntled investors for centuries. The difference is that the occurrence is now more frequent, as are the successes.

There are two main reasons for the increase in broker litigation. First, society has become more litigious. It is a symptom of the times that people seem to be more prone to fight, to go to court. Successful suits against brokers are well published and often enjoy stature as a triumph of David over Goliath. Lawyers advertise for clients with complaints. In certain jurisdictions contingency arrangements are allowed (the lawyer receives a portion of any settlement or award as his fee) and a number of lawyers are busy building

7

reputations as "broker bashers."

The second reason for the increasing number of lawsuits is directly related to the complexity of the broker's job and the difficulty of knowing when it has been carried out completely. This latter development is a product of job evolution. It has been fostered in part by a competitive drive to provide the customer with more and more service for the purpose of eliciting his business. It may be ironic, but a broker may find himself on the defendant's end of a lawsuit simply for fostering trust and reliance, the very essence of the relationship he has tried to create.

The complexities mount. Firms' compliance manuals become law by adoption of the courts. Complaints to dealer associations initiate costly, probative investigations. The advent of the "discount" broker will cause problems. If the full service brokers are charging more, they must be giving something more. Court decisions keep pounding at the fine lines distinguishing financial advisors from analysts from brokers. Short of becoming a lawyer or seeking counsel on every order, what is a broker, a producer, to do?

That was the dilemma that I began to address in my first presentations to brokers. This guide, by combining a working understanding of the basis for liability and some practical solutions, is meant to alleviate some of the problem.

Bill, on his first day, is introduced to his manager, compliance officer and lawyer.

THE EVOLUTION

The Rhoads *case epitomizes the evolution in the law concerning broker liability. In the one case three major issues leading to broker liability are examined. But* Rhoads *does not enunciate new law, it merely examines well-established legal principles.*

Of the three components to the solution - understanding the origins of liability, an analysis of the relationship, and a practical plan for reducing risk - the first is perhaps most important. Understanding how and why liability arises is the first step towards avoiding it.

In order to obtain the knowledge of where liability arises and dispel some common misconceptions it is useful to look at one or two cases that have epitomized the evolution in broker liability.

Mr. and Mrs. Rhoads - The Evidence

Few cases are more illustrative than *Rhoads v. Prudential-Bache Securities Canada Ltd. et al.* The decision is the subject of a great deal of controversy in the securities industry, and reaction varies from disbelief to shock, depending on which version of the evidence is discussed.

Before proceeding to discuss the facts of *Rhoads*, it is important to distinguish between "evidence" and "facts." Since later we will be concerning ourselves with providing *evidence* that certain duties have been fulfilled so that a judge can find certain *facts* in our favour, it is worth a short digression into the world of Perry Mason. Apart from casting light on the *Rhoads* case, understanding the distinction makes a popular monotony breaker at tedious cocktail parties (try, "We heard the evidence of Anita Hill and the evidence of Clarence Thomas, but what were the facts?")

There was a great deal of conflicting evidence in *Rhoads*. At trial the judge heard the brokers give evidence that conflicted with the evidence given by the plaintiffs, Mr. and Mrs. Rhoads. In my discussions with members of the industry, particularly with those most appalled by the result, more often than not reference is made to some conflicting evidence.

To come to a decision the judge had to reconcile the conflicting evidence. He had to consider the best evidence available, including the demeanour and credibility of the witnesses, the consistency of their stories, and supporting evidence. At the end of the day he had to decide what he believed to be true and resolve certain matters by coming to a conclusion as to what portions of the conflicting evidence he accepted. This is known in legal parlance as "making a finding of fact." It was on those facts, as he found them, that his legal conclusions were based. The Court of Appeal, which does not hear the witnesses, is bound (other than in exceptional circumstances) to accept the facts as found by the trial judge, who was in a position to weigh the evidence. Despite the conflicting evidence, the *Rhoads* decision was based on certain findings of fact, and we will for our discussion focus only on the facts as the judge found them in order to understand the decision.

The Rhoads were a retired couple who had moved to Victoria after selling their business in the United States. Having little or no investment experience they attended a free investment seminar conducted by the Yzenbrandts on behalf of Prudential- Bache. After listening to Mr. and Mrs. Yzenbrandt, who were respectively the branch manager and a broker at the local Bache office, Mr. and Mrs. Rhoads met with Mrs. Yzenbrandt to discuss their needs further.

The Rhoads explained to Mrs. Yzenbrandt that they had minimal investment experience. What they wanted was someone to look over their investments, advise them on prudent choices in keeping with their investment objectives and keep them posted on matters affecting their portfolio.

In addition the Rhoads told Mrs. Yzenbrandt they were retired and had to have a certain amount of monthly income from their investment to maintain their lifestyle.

In response Mrs. Yzenbrandt stressed her experience, and the reputation of Prudential Bache - the "rock." She then discussed equity mutual funds. She assured the Rhoads that they were safe, that they would only fluctuate a "penny or two." The Rhoads were told that the risk warnings on the prospectuses they were given were a legal requirement. They were told to concentrate on the track record of the funds invested.

Thus reassured, the Rhoads invested the bulk of their life savings, some $600,000, in equity mutual funds and some preferred shares and treasury bills.

Some time later the Rhoads went on a holiday, leaving a telephone number by which Mrs. Yzenbrandt could contact them if necessary. While the Rhoads were on holiday, Mr. Yzenbrandt, the branch manager, wrote and mailed a letter to all branch clients. In it he warned of negative market indicators and suggested selling all common and preferred shares, as well as equity mutual funds. A copy of the letter was sent to the Rhoads' home address. No effort was made to contact them through the number left with Mrs. Yzenbrandt.

The Rhoads did not return from their holiday until October 14, 1987 and did not read their mail, including Mr. Yzenbrandts' letter, for a few days. Concerned about the contents of the letter, they attended the Bache offices on October 19, 1987, "Black Monday." Notwithstanding the market was dropping rapidly, the Yzenbrandts had no advice for the Rhoads. When they again attended on the Yzenbrandts on the 24th of October they were told that Bache had $300,000-a-year vice-presidents in Toronto who did not know what to do. Not receiving any advice, the Rhoads liquidated their position, incurring losses in excess of $132,000.

Mr. and Mrs. Rhoads - The Decision

In January of 1991, in a decision upheld by the Court of Appeal, the Supreme Court of British Columbia awarded damages against Prudential-Bache and the Yzenbrandts for the amount of the loss plus interest and costs.

What had happened? How could brokers who sold good, solid mutual funds and some preferred shares end up responsible for losses that occurred over the infamous "Black Monday?"

The decision has understandably created a great deal of consternation in the industry. In particular, plaintiffs' lawyers will certainly continue to cite *Rhoads* in support of their clients' position that their losses should be recoverable. However, concerns that a new and unwieldy level of financial responsibility is being imposed on brokers are lessened when the component elements of the decision are examined.

Rhoads merely incorporated existing jurisprudence dealing with broker responsibility. With its particular facts *Rhoads* may seem a controversial decision. But the *Rhoads* decision was based on the same fundamental principles applicable to almost all broker liability cases and thus makes a good starting point for a discussion of those principles.

Mr. and Mrs. Rhoads - The Reasons

The court in *Rhoads* found liability on three grounds - three elements that are almost always examined in a broker-client dispute. They are breach of contract, negligence and breach of fiduciary duty.

In determining that there had been a breach of contract, the court looked at the Rhoads' stated objective, that of secure monthly income. The judge rejected defence testimony that the Rhoads were aware of the "encroachment clause" enabling cash flow to be sustained by sale of shares. There was expert opinion that the selection of equity mutual funds, rather than income-based funds, was inappropriate to meet their income objectives. Accordingly, the defendants were liable because the Rhoads did not receive that for which they had contracted, namely, investments to meet their income objective.

The negligence occurred through the Yzenbrandts' failure to comply with industry standards. Those failures were not observing the "know your client rule" by Mrs. Yzenbrandt for not taking more than a cursory interest in the clients' account application, and Mr. Yzenbrandt's failure to adequately comply with his supervisory duties of reviewing the new account and the subsequent investments.

Finally, because the Rhoads had placed their trust and reliance on the Yzenbrandts, the court found a fiduciary relationship existed. The existence of a fiduciary relationship had placed an onus on the Yzenbrandts to advise the plaintiffs fully, honestly and in good faith, to carry out their intentions. The duties attendant on this relationship were breached when equity mutual funds were recommended as opposed to income funds, and again when the Rhoads were not contacted after Mr. Yzenbrandt issued his market-warning letter.

The End of the Line?

Did the *Rhoads* case make new law? Not really. On first hearing of it, many brokers assumed *Rhoads* was setting a precedent for a new level of broker responsibility. However, when made aware of the facts, brokers seem less troubled by the outcome.

The judge in *Rhoads* did not have to enunciate new principles. For each area of responsibility he drew on existing law and applied the jurisprudence to the facts, as he found them. While there is some controversy over the evidence (a good lesson to bear in mind when we talk about evidence later), once the facts are accepted, the decision is not altogether surprising.

One feature of *Rhoads* is that it discusses three elements of broker liability - breach of contract, negligence, and breach of fiduciary duty. The conclusions reached in *Rhoads*, and the discussion of the jurisprudence contained in the lengthy trial decision are useful illustrations of the state of the law. Consequently, the case is a handy stepping-off point for discussion. *Rhoads* also makes a handy guide (unfortunately) for plaintiffs' lawyers. Statements of claim

16

I have received recently seem like a cut-and-paste workover of *Rhoads*.

However, each new case will present new facts; some significantly different, others with only subtle nuances to distinguish the situation. How a judge will apply the law to the variation in facts remains to be seen. What is important however, is that *Rhoads* is largely representative of the evolution of the law to date and a basis for future development. The principles contained therein however will likely remain germane for some time.

THE ELEMENTS

Broker liability generally results from failings in one of three areas. The component elements of the common causes of action, the "ought to's" vary with the relationship the broker has with his client. Understanding the source of obligations is more helpful than lists of duties.

Broker liability encompasses more than one legal cause of action. It is a generic term referring to situations where a broker must pay for losses arising out of one or more breaches of legal responsibility. These generally fall into one of three categories: breach of contract, negligence, and breach of fiduciary duty.

It is not the intention that this guide become a treatise on those legal issues. Apart from lawyers, few people have the need, inclination or patience to absorb the extensive jurisprudence related to them.

Still, if we are to avoid liability, we need a good handle on how it arises. To that end, it is useful to examine sources of broker liability in its component elements.

The "Ought To's"

We can, for functional purposes, reduce a great deal of legal jargon down to "ought to." For all the fancy terms coined, the pervasive legal hazard faced by a broker is failing to do

18

something he "ought to" have done. The significance of the legal terms such as "negligence" and "breach of fiduciary duty," is that the breach of those obligations gives rise to liability. But in the final analysis they still amount to a court-sanctioned list of "ought to's." The purpose of our examination of the legal principles involved will be to learn what the "ought to's" are, and when they arise.

Breach of Contract

One of the more common pleadings in broker liability suits is breach of contract. A plea of breach of contract is simply an allegation that the broker did not provide his client with what he "ought to" have, based on what the client had contracted to receive.

The contract, that is the engagement for the broker's services, has two kinds of terms: those in the written agreements, (the account forms, margin agreements and the like) and unwritten terms, which are made up of implied terms and oral promises.

The breach of either written or unwritten terms can result in liability, but it is the latter that is more problematic. After all, if we are trying to ascertain what we ought to be doing to fulfil our contractual obligations, we should know what the terms of the contract are.

The Written Contract

The written contract takes the form of all the agreements executed by the client with the brokerage firm. Usually it is comprised of various documents such as account forms, joint account forms, margin account agreements and the like. The thrust of most of them is to set out the manner in which the firm and its employee brokers will buy, sell and hold the client's securities and funds.

Because the terms are written, and because many of the forms are standard and in widespread use, the written contracts do not usually give the broker problems. That is not to say that a broker should not be familiar with them - a breach can result in liability. Furthermore, they can be a two-edged sword in that terms that appear to be in the firm's interest can still result in liability when breached by its employee, the broker.

Consider the case where a margin account agreement provided for margin calls and subsequent liquidation if the call was not met. The courts have considered that not giving a margin call but simply meeting the deficiency by drawing from another of the client's accounts was denying the client a contractual right he had to review his options when the call should have been made!

Just because written terms are less frequently the subject of debate than unwritten terms does not mean the written contract should be ignored.

The Unwritten Terms

What then are the unwritten terms? The implied terms include obligations incidental to your engagement, to your basic role, that of buying and selling securities. As part of your contract, your engagement to buy and sell, it is an implied term that you will provide your services within the confines of the rules and regulations under which the industry operates. Accordingly, orders must be entered in compliance with stock exchange bylaws of which your firm is a member. Not only are you obligated to do so, your client is bound to accept the consequences of complying with these rules. In one case a client was not allowed to cancel his "market opening" order after an announcement of a delayed market opening because his broker (and therefore the client), was bound by The Toronto Stock Exchange bylaws prohibiting a change after the delayed opening was announced.

Along with your obligation to fill orders there is an implied term that you will do so in a timely fashion, and report appropriately.

As well as considering terms incidental to any written arrangements it is necessary to see if you have contracted to do something more through any verbal arrangement.

Herein lay the rub in *Rhoads*. It became clear that the Rhoads, who had little investment experience, sought the help of the Yzenbrandts to suggest investments to them that would meet certain criteria, specifically income. In other words, the broker was not simply being engaged to buy and sell stock; the deal was to buy and sell a certain kind of security. That was a term of the contract, something the broker "ought to" have done.

Not every representation becomes a term of contract. A representation that is not a term of contract does not result in liability if it is breached. The difficulty arises in knowing when such representation becomes an enforceable obligation, to which liability attaches.

Statements such as "I'll call you with interesting situations" or "I'll give you great service" may result in a loss of a client for failure to perform, but are likely too unspecific, or uncertain, to be construed as a term of contract. However, a client may very well impute into a contract a term that the broker will only recommend investments that produce income (as in *Rhoads*), or say, bear dividends, or have tax advantages. Accordingly, brokers have been found liable for losses occurring when certain investments were handled in a way that did not provide the tax treatment the client had specified was essential. That request had been a term of contract, the breach of which resulted in liability.

That is not to say that the broker guarantees performance. We will consider the broker's obligation to make inquiries when we deal with negligence. However, the broker should not be liable if say, he was to buy dividend bearing preferred shares in accordance with his client's instructions, and sometime later the corporation becomes unable to pay the dividends. The broker has delivered what he was contracted to do - buy preferred shares. He has not guaranteed results of the investment.

A representation becomes a term of the contract if it goes to the root of the relationship. To determine whether something is a term of contract it is useful to ask whether the relationship would have been entered into without it. If the Rhoads had been told that the Yzenbrandts would be purchasing securities other that those that met their income criteria, it is likely they would not have entered into the relationship. Accordingly, purchasing income producing securities was a term of the contract.

In brief then, the "ought to's" that arise under contract include the obligation to do all the things specified in the written agreement, all the things that are normal and incidental to performing those obligations, and anything else that the client has bargained to obtain and which goes to the root of the relationship.

Negligence

The second ground for broker liability is negligence. Negligence has had much written about it, and while it is presumptuous to try and reduce the jurisprudence to one line, the concept can be grasped by stating that when you have a relationship with someone, whether contractual, financial, even physical, you have a duty to behave in a certain way towards that person. When you do not behave that way you have been negligent. If your failure to behave that way causes loss, and that loss was foreseeable, you are liable.

In other words, there are certain things you ought to do, depending on how the obligation arises. For instance, if you are a cab driver, you ought to obey the rules of the road; if a doctor, you ought to check to see if all clamps are removed before sewing up your patient; if a lawyer, you ought to file a statement of claim before the limitation date has expired.

The difficulty, once the existence of a relationship has been established, is in determining what duties or obligations exist. Obviously the broker in a relationship with his client needs to know what those duties, or "ought to's" are so he can determine whether he has completed his job.

Outlining the standard of conduct required in various relationships has taken up considerable amounts of the court's time and resulted in volumes of case reports containing their discussions.

The Reasonable Man

For assistance in establishing what conduct was acceptable in various circumstances, the courts created a new individual, the "reasonable man" (for history buffs, the "man on the Clapham omnibus.")

To establish whether a duty had been discharged, the court would ask, "What would a reasonable man do in this situation?"

The courts then further refined the reasonable man as an individual who had all the skills and knowledge that came with his position. For instance, in medical matters the question was what a reasonable doctor would do in the situation; for shipping, the reasonable captain was the test; at law, the reasonable lawyer, and so on.

The courts, while sometimes considering themselves all-knowing, generally recognized they did not have the expertise to know what the reasonable man of various professions would do in each case, so they would seek help on the point. That help would take the form of experts.

"Experts" are people qualified to give testimony as to what is an acceptable standard of conduct in any particular industry. For the purposes of a trial a court will accept as expert evidence that testimony from an individual whose experience and standing in the profession should, in the court's view, qualify his opinions on matters as acceptable. Obviously, greater experience and qualifications are important.

In broker liability suits, plaintiffs often provide their own experts - sometimes officers from other brokerage firms, compliance managers or consultants. If the court accepts that the expert is qualified to give an opinion, it generally will not replace that expert's opinion with its own view of what would amount to reasonable conduct.

Accordingly, your standard of conduct will be set by your peers, that is, by your colleagues in the industry, testifying as to what is acceptable practice in the industry.

Industry Guidelines

The court will also note an industry's own guidelines in establishing sufficiency of conduct. In determining if a defendant has discharged his duty, that is, has done what a reasonable man would in the situation, the court will look to prescribed guidelines or industry standards to assess his conduct. In other words, as far as the court is concerned, the reasonable broker is one who conducts his affairs in accordance with his industry's accepted guidelines. Accordingly, the reasonable broker conducts his affairs as set out in his compliance manual.

This point bears emphasis. A broker who violates one of the industry's accepted operating standards may get away with it, in that it is not detected, or causes no immediate consequence. He may not have broken a law *per se*. But if he ends up facing a claim by a disgruntled client for negligence, be assured that the plaintiff's lawyer will turn that divergence from guidelines into a major headache when trying to establish conduct as a reasonable broker.

The Yzenbrandts discovered this in the *Rhoads* case. Mr. Justice Cohen, in finding the defendants negligent, stated, "On the whole of the evidence, I am satisfied that had industry standards been complied with, the plaintiffs would not have sustained their losses." He then writes three pages considering the "know your client" rule.

In the case of Mr. Yzenbrandt, the court simply cites two regulations requiring new account forms to be approved by a senior official and investments reviewed for suitability. Mr. Yzenbrandt, the branch manager, in failing to have done so, is found negligent. Mr. Justice Cohen did not have to create a list of duties for the reasonable branch manager - the industry itself prescribed such obligations.

Accordingly, "know your client" and "suitability," cardinal rules in the industry, became court-directed "ought to's."

Another example of the courts adopting industry standards is *Varcoe v. Sterling, Dean Witter et al.* In that Ontario case, a knowledgeable futures trader was allowed to exceed the dealer's own guidelines, contained in its manual, as to trading limits. As a consequence, Dean Witter was found liable for a substantial loss when a large position in Standard & Poors 500 index which the client purchased hit the skids.

In Ontario, under the Commodity Futures Act, dealers are required to file and receive approval of a compliance manual that, among other things, establishes guidelines for determining a client's suitability for trading. Once filed, generally regulatory bodies do not review activities for ongoing adherence.

In *Varcoe* the court recognized that the regulations imposed a special duty of care toward commodity clients in light of the high degree of risk and potential for huge loss. Accordingly, brokerage firms were to have compliance manuals setting out suitability provisions. The regulations were, in the view of the court, for the benefit of the client.

Therefore, the court concluded "A broker who violates his own self proclaimed rules and exposes the customer to a higher degree of risk is in breach of that duty of care."

The case is driven to some degree by its unusual facts, but it still fits within our "ought to" analysis.

The commodity broker "ought to" have behaved as a reasonable commodity broker would in the situation. Such a broker would exercise care in handling the client's account to ensure that the client did not exceed the firm's own guidelines as to suitability.

It is interesting that the decision did not have to be based on a discussion of suitability. The experience of the customer - a retired lawyer with extensive trading experience and significant means - might have been reason for considerable debate on the point. But the courts are not interested in replacing established standards with their own. In *Varcoe* there were set guidelines, and those guidelines were violated. The verdict was negligence.

So the courts have another source of establishing what amounts to reasonable conduct by a broker - his firm's own codes or guidelines of conduct. Those guidelines are very likely to be accepted as "ought to's" by the courts, and a broker ignoring them does so at his peril.

Misrepresentation

While we have examined negligence in the context of a relationship giving rise to "ought to's" it is arguable that there are some "ought to *not*" items on the list, most notably not make negligent misrepresentation.

For consistency, however, liability for negligent misrepresentation or misstatement can still be considered an "ought to" - a broker ought to be reasonably certain about any representations he makes.

Liability for negligent misrepresentation comes under the heading of "negligence" because it concerns a duty that arises out of a relationship. In a broker-client relationship it can be anticipated that a client will act on a broker's representations, for example, a "tip." If the tip is wrong, it is foreseeable that the client could lose money. Hence, the broker has a duty of care, an "ought to" to ensure that he does not make any such representation outside the standards applicable to reasonable conduct.

Repeating conclusions from a firm's research department accordingly would be within the realm of reasonable conduct. But news spilled over a few drinks by some lower-level company executive? Try to imagine how you could establish that it was the conduct of a reasonable broker to pass on such information without qualification.

Foreseeability

Finally, to be liable for damages in negligence, the loss must have been a foreseeable consequence of the breach of duty. Foreseeability has occupied a great deal of space in the texts and cases dealing with negligence, and is the subject of some great jurisprudential debate. (Example, is a second ship catching fire in a harbour a foreseeable consequence of a negligent act that caused a first ship to catch fire? Seriously, cases like this are discussed extensively!)

The loss must be a foreseeable consequence of the negligent act, not of the future in general. A broker who recommends well-researched blue-chip stocks in keeping with his client's objectives has not committed a negligent act, if, for reasons not known to him at the time, the industry later suffers a turn-around and the particular stock suffers. In contrast, passing on an unfounded "tip" without qualification is negligent. An easily foreseeable consequence of such a negligent act is that the tip may prove untrue, and the stock decline.

Unfortunately, when a broker has been negligent, financial loss is almost always a foreseeable consequence. Accordingly, the issue of foreseeability is not frequently going to assist a broker in avoiding liability for a negligent act.

I always buy on my broker's tips. If the stocks go up, I make money. If they go down, I sue him.

Fiduciary Duty

Few areas of concern will be more problematic to a broker than establishing whether he has a fiduciary relationship with his client, and determining if he has discharged the duties attendant on that relationship.

From the plaintiff's perspective, to be able to allege breach of fiduciary duty is truly a cannon in his arsenal of weapons.

In its simplest dictionary meaning "fiduciary" is an adjective meaning given, or held, in trust. As a noun, it is trustee, from the Latin *fiducia*, trust. Standing in a fiduciary position gives rise to further legal responsibility based on the concept of trust.

If the idea of negligence is difficult to reduce to one line, fiduciary duty is even trickier. Still, the idea can be kept relatively simple if thought of as a situation where there are a few more "ought to's."

The reason there are more, or different (some would say "higher") duties, is a result of the nature of the relationship with the client. If a broker has a fiduciary relationship with his client, that is, if he is in the position of a fiduciary, he will have fiduciary duties ("ought to's") which, if not performed, can give rise to liability.

Two questions then obviously arise - when does a fiduciary relationship exist and what are the corresponding obligations?

32

It is perhaps easier to give a short answer to the second question. The broker who is in the position of a fiduciary to his client has an obligation to advise that client carefully, fully, honestly and in good faith and to carry out the client's intention. In doing so, he must exercise skill and diligence appropriate to the situation.

The question of whether one is a fiduciary, is more problematic and, as the cases confirm, the answer depends on the facts in each situation. However, if we can grasp the essentials of a fiduciary relationship, we may be a little more sensitive to its presence.

It is well established that not every client-broker relationship is fiduciary. However, with the increasing complexity of the profession, the relationship is occurring more frequently.

The essence of a fiduciary relationship is a situation where one person trusts another to do something, or take care of something, and in so doing makes it clear that he is either unable, or unwilling, to independently verify that the other person is carrying out that trust. That other person must have accepted that trust, either expressly or implicitly, knowing if he does not fulfil his trust, the first person is vulnerable and liable to be hurt.

Mr. Justice Cohen in *Rhoads* stated "The key factor in establishing a fiduciary relationship is where one person is vulnerable to another and is liable to be hurt if the first person breaches the trust reposed in him."

In *Rhoads*, the Yzenbrandts had invited Mr. and Mrs. Rhoads to entrust them with looking after their investment goals. The Yzenbrandts assured the Rhoads they could do so and stressed their experience and the reputation of Prudential Bache. The Rhoads were looking for advice and Mrs. Yzenbrandt knew the plaintiffs were seeking the benefit of her best skills.

From this we glean two elements: a trusting or reliance on someone and a vulnerability or possibility of being hurt by the person trusted if the trust is not carried out.

Other cases and texts stress the same elements, with one author stating, "Vulnerability, arising through justifiable reliance or in some other way, is at the root of liability for breach of fiduciary obligation."

When a customer is relying on a broker for something, and when he does not have the independent means to verify what the broker is doing, or alternatively does not do so because he believes the broker is carrying out the trust and exercising his skills at appropriate levels, he is vulnerable. If the broker accepts that responsibility, he will be liable for losses occasioned by his failure to discharge the responsibility he has accepted.

As stated, not all relationships are fiduciary. It is interesting that in the *Varcoe* case the court found that there was no fiduciary relationship between Varcoe and his broker, Sterling. Notwithstanding that Varcoe consulted with Sterling on many trades, and had a high level of respect for

Sterling's skill and knowledge as well as confidence in his opinions, the court focused on the fact that there was no reliance placed by Varcoe on Sterling's advice. There was, in the words of the court, "... no transfer of any power to Sterling which would make Varcoe vulnerable."

A word of caution here. *Varcoe* should not be interpreted as standing for the proposition that when an order has originated from a client, or the purchase was a decision left up to the client, a fiduciary relationship does not exist. Varcoe was a sophisticated trader, a retired lawyer who had traded in speculative stocks and futures extensively with Sterling and others. He was initiating trades, originating ideas and was not looking to Sterling for advice, at least not to the level of reliance. A client who is knowledgeable may still be reposing trust in his broker and accordingly open the door to fiduciary responsibility.

Duties of the Fiduciary

Once the relationship of fiduciary has been established - the client has placed trust in the hands of a broker, who has accepted the responsibility - additional duties or "ought to's" are triggered.

On an examination of those duties - to advise carefully, fully, honestly and in good faith, and carry out the client's intention - we do not see so much a different duty or "ought to" in kind; the difference is more in scope. Even the application of a quality element - appropriate skill and diligence - are not new or different from the "ought to's"

35

that a reasonable broker exercises to avoid negligence.

What is different is the scope of the duties, that is, the number of "ought to's" that apply to the situation. This increase in obligations is a direct result of the specific trust placed in the broker's hands.

Accordingly, if a client is trusting and relying on the broker to find income investments, he must do so. If the mandate is to find "ultra-conservative" investments, the broker in a fiduciary relationship must exercise his skills at the highest level applicable to his profession to carry out his client's intention. If the client has entrusted the broker to warn of unusual market conditions, that is an extra duty, an additional "ought to" that a broker has in that fiduciary relationship.

When the broker has accepted the additional duty, it is no answer to say the client could have taken care of the matter himself. The duty arises by virtue of the broker knowing the client has entrusted something to his care and accepting that trust. Taking care of the matter in accordance with applicable professional standards is the only means by which the broker discharges the obligation.

COMPLETING THE ELEMENTS

Understanding the component elements that give rise to broker liability is only part of the solution. Knowing when they arise, and how the obligations are discharged, is the other part. Lists of duties can never be exhaustive. It is more important to understand how the duties arise in a particular broker-client relationship so that the broker will know when his job is completed.

A Brief Review

In our quest to understand where liability arises we have looked at the component elements of broker liability. We have seen that they come under the headings of breach of contract, negligence, and breach of fiduciary duty.

In each case we have viewed the components as giving rise to "ought to's." In contract, a broker ought to do what he has been contracted to do. To avoid negligence, he ought to use the skill and care a reasonable broker would use. Finally, for those who have entered into a fiduciary relationship, they ought to advise carefully, fully and honestly, in good faith, and carry out the client's intention, while exercising skill and diligence.

However, it is one thing to understand the component elements, but the broker who wants to sleep well at night wants to know, before the matter reaches litigation, whether he has completed them.

It is trite to say "do your job." Figuring out just what the job is, and whether the component elements have been completed is often the very issue at the heart of broker liability suits.

Figuring Out The Job

Since we have discovered that being a broker means being different things to different people, and more importantly, that as the relationship changes so do obligations, it is important to review the relationship the broker has with the client.

There is a sliding scale of broker-client relationships. At the one end there is the broker *simpliciter*, for example, being on the receiving end of an unsolicited order (and even that has responsibilities), to the other end of the scale, that of a position of trust as a fiduciary. As the consequences of each of these relationships vary, it is important to be able to quantify the depth of the relationship.

Furthermore, bear in mind that if a problem arises the client will have a say as to how he viewed his relationship. Generally speaking it will be in his interest to increase the complexity of the relationship and hence the duties and responsibilities. Your assessment of your relationship should be as objective as possible. Do the reasonable man test - how would he view your relationship and responsibilities. Note here I did not say "reasonable broker" since your client is unlikely to be a broker. If it is reasonable for the client to believe that you have accepted a higher responsibility, a court may very well find that you have.

A good approach, other than asking yourself "What's my relationship with this customer?" is to view the relationship from several angles. Consider the reason the customer is using you. Has he asked you to do something more than fill an order? Ask yourself if there is something unique expected of you, or could he just as well be serviced by anyone else in the office.

If you are going to err, be on the safe side and assume there is more, not less, of a relationship.

When you are comfortable with your assessment of the relationship, then sit back and, within the framework of the three headings of potential liability, ask yourself "What ought I be doing here?" The "checklist" in the next chapter can help.

Furthermore, don't forget that relationships change. As time goes on you will become more familiar with the client - likely a desired result. Just bear in mind that as his trust and reliance on you grows, so does the complexity of the relationship and the possibility of increased responsibility on your part.

Completing the Contract

As we have already noted, there are written and unwritten terms of a contract, and it is the latter that is more problematic. However, that is not to say the written contract is to be ignored.

To determine what your obligations are under the written contract, read it. A contract is an agreement to do certain things, which if not done, can give rise to damages. The measure of damages under law of contract is to put the aggrieved party in the position he would have been had the contract been properly carried out. Accordingly, even little slip-ups can cost big. If your account form says you will promptly give your client notice of an undermargin situation and you don't, you can bet that if a problem arises he will argue that you breached your obligation and he is not responsible for any loss from the time he should have been called. Read the contract and be familiar with its obligations.

The other terms of contract are unwritten and come about principally in two ways: by implication and by oral representations.

Implied Terms

When carrying out a contract as a member firm of a stock exchange, the firm is bound by rules of the exchange, and it is implied that in fulfilling your contract, you will do so within the applicable rules of the exchange. Furthermore, the courts will also find that it is an implied term of contract to conduct your business in accordance with industry practice.

Accordingly, if you are not complying with an exchange rule or regulation, you are breaching an implied term of contract. This does not necessarily work against the broker, and the broker is entitled to adhere to such rules, as did the broker who refused to cancel a market order after an announcement of a delayed opening. He was merely complying with an implied term of his contract - that is that the rules of the exchange applied. To digress from exchange rules and industry practice is to open the door to risk.

Most brokers are familiar with exchange rules and conduct business within industry practice - or at least their compliance officers encourage them to. In every situation ask yourself if you are complying with those implied terms. If not, a red flag should go up immediately. If anything goes wrong, it will not be very difficult to assess liability.

Oral Terms

More trouble arises when the term of contract allegedly breached is an oral one. The risks are obvious. In most cases only two people are aware of any such terms - the broker and the client - and the judge will have to decide whom he believes.

Questions of evidence aside for the moment, a more

pressing issue is, whether in the course of your contact with your client, you have created an additional term of contract, the breach of which may result in liability.

In your discussions with clients representations of various sorts will be made. Yes, you'll keep an eye out for good buys, or yes you will send him some company's brochure, or maybe you'll call him with interesting information about new companies. Not all representations become a term of contract.

As a broker you are contracted to buy and sell stocks, and, as we have seen, part of that contract is the implication that you will do so in accordance with exchange rules and industry practice. However, your obligations may be broader if you have contracted to do something further. In *Rhoads*, the Yzenbrandts were found to have contracted to purchase securities that met with the clients' requirements.

How do you establish whether you have contracted to give your customer something more, something that is a term of contract? One approach is to consider whether the client is using you as a broker because you offered that extra something. This is not a foolproof test, but consider that if the answer is "yes" you can be sure the client will argue there was that additional contractual obligation.

Failing to provide good service may lose the client, but that will not necessarily result in liability unless there was some more specific obligation. Offering to call someone in advance of some event however may become a term of contract. You must consider whether the existence of the representation in question is part of the relationship - would your relationship with the client exist if he were told that you would not perform the matter in question. Does it go to the root of your arrangement?

Remember, when a representation is found to be a term of contract and it is breached, for whatever reason, there is liability, and if loss, damages. It matters not, when a contract is breached, what the circumstances leading to the breach were. Acting reasonably in the circumstances may be a defense to negligence, but not to breach of contract. If you have promised to do something, and that promise is a term of contract, do it.

Avoiding Negligence

We have already reduced, for discussion purposes, the concept of negligence to one line, namely, that once in a relationship with someone, a person has a duty to behave in a certain way. The duty of the broker is to behave as a reasonable broker.

Can we prepare a catalogue of how a reasonable broker behaves? The answer is "yes" to some degree, although there would be limits on the usefulness of the exercise.

One limitation of such a catalogue is that it would be impossible to anticipate every situation. Not all scenarios have been considered by the courts and many decisions are not helpful in that they deal with very peculiar facts.

Another limitation is related to the object of this guide - to assist in reducing risk without interfering with production. I can think of few things more damaging than giving an epistle of conduct judicially considered for a broker to review.

The better approach is to understand the concept, namely, that the basis for liability is a broker's failure to conduct himself in a certain manner. Accordingly, when a broker conducts himself in a manner that puts a client at risk and that action, or lack of action as the case may be, is outside of the realm of conduct of a reasonable broker, he has breached his duty.

In reviewing your activities, rather than comparing your conduct with a list of everything you could possibly do, consider whether you have done in each case what a reasonable broker would have done.

We keep coming back to the "reasonable broker" and what he would do but hopefully this is not drawing too many blank stares. As a broker you have had professional training and deal with other professionals. Accordingly, you have the knowledge and skill, or access to the resources, that would give you the power to think like the reasonable broker.

The reasonable broker is not implied to have magic vision or omnipotence; rather he is an individual who is vested with the skill and knowledge attributable to his profession and one who exercises his craft accordingly.

Thus, for example, the court found a broker liable for losses incurred through writing naked options without explaining the risks adequately. The court found the reasonable broker would have taken steps to see the client understood the high risk.

In another case a broker had passed on a tip, based on questionable information, about an oil find that ultimately proved untrue. The broker was found liable in negligence for failing to ascertain the facts with reasonable accuracy. The reasonable broker, knowing his client would act on the tip, would have taken steps to verify the information, or at least warned of the risks associated with the quality of the information.

In yet another situation, a broker had released a preliminary report of his research department. The client acted on it, losing money. The final version of the report noted concerns not contained in the preliminary release. Leaving alone the question of whether the reasonable analyst would put a preliminary report in the hands of a broker (he probably would not), the broker could have saved himself some grief. He may not have had specific industry guidelines or regulations dealing with the situation, but he could have considered what a reasonable broker "ought to" do with the report. If he had doubts, he could have discussed the situation with his office manager or other professionals. Remember your fellow professionals can be an asset in determining acceptable practice.

In consulting others, however, do not gloss over your considerations or take a quick consensus view. Often, when faced with a decision regarding conduct, brokers will bounce a question off the broker at the next desk. Considered opinions of competent colleagues can indeed give comfort that you are acting reasonably. But a quick consensus view does not replace thinking the question through, carefully, as a professional applying all his skill to the situation.

Consider too the implication of your acting or failing to act. We have seen that foreseeability of loss is an essential element to attaching liability to negligence. If you are struggling with a particular point, try reversing the question. Before considering whether something is a duty, ask yourself if you omit to do that something, is loss to your client foreseeable? If the answer is "yes" it may make you reconsider whether it is something a reasonable broker "ought to" do.

The "Imposed" Duties

Know your client, and review suitability. These two obligations appear here in a discussion of negligence because they are duties, and when a duty is breached, we have negligence.

We have already discussed the origins of the duties and their embodiment through regulatory sanction and the courts as an element of professional obligation, so there is little need to argue their existence. What is needed is an understanding of when these duties are fulfilled.

Know Your Client

Let's look first at "Know Your Client." It is the one rule subjected to scrutiny perhaps more than any other, yet, in my view, one of the easier obligations to fulfil. In truth, most brokers know their client far better than any client application form would indicate and that is a very important problem of evidence.

The hard evidence most brokers have that they know their client is the initial client application form. The Registered Representative manual provides a form, the "New Client Application Form," which is in widespread use. Often, regulations requiring prudent business practices and supervision declare that those regulations, to the extent that they involve making enquiries to know the client, have been complied with by using approved forms.

While completing the form may initially comply with regulations and is undoubtedly standard practice, it is of itself, in my view, inadequate in complying with the obligation to "know your client." There are several reasons.

The main problem is that in its present form the new client application form just does not demonstrate adequately that you know your client. The information to be put in the small blanks is far short of what would adequately demonstrate an understanding of your client, his fiscal

47

objectives and capacities. The expert witness in the *Rhoads* case listed some thirty questions that should be answered to "know your client."

Another problem arising from the inadequacy of the form is that it gives very little assistance in determining the client's investment objectives. Breaking goals down to five categories is gross oversimplification. And the ambiguity can backfire. More than once I have seen several "experts" disagree as to which category a particular stock would belong. Furthermore, the form does not give a concrete indication of the client's appetite for risk.

For longer term clients the new client account forms are seldom a reflection of reality after the passage of time. Assets and incomes change, but more importantly, with experience and time, so does the client's approach to investing, and his objectives.

No one argues with the "know your client" concept. The cases have shown you need more than just a hazy idea about your client's fiscal background. However, the limited information on the application form may lead to an erroneous conclusion that is indeed all you have.

If the client turns the matter over to his lawyer the first thing he will request is a copy of the client's application form. In most cases the form will suggest that the broker had only a very limited idea about his client. And with the ambiguous characterization of objectives, it is not that difficult to argue that a broker has little evidence of compliance with the cardinal "ought to" of knowing his client.

Here is one very important point that may not readily come to mind for the non-lawyer. When the plaintiff's lawyer sees the new account application form, that is generally all the evidence he has as to how well the broker complied with the "know your client" rule. His only other information about the case is what his client told him. His client of course is interested in seeing his case go forward, and, notwithstanding the folly of explaining only favourable facts to your lawyer, that is what most clients do to varying extremes. Unless the client has been unusually forthright in explaining the total relationship he had with his broker, the plaintiff's lawyer may well consider that the limited information on the form is the extent of the broker's knowledge of the client, his financial background, and objectives. And, if the plaintiff's lawyer has a good understanding of what "know your client" means (or has considered the expert testimony in *Rhoads*) he will very likely believe he has a good case.

From our perspective we want the matter to go away at the earliest possible stage. The plaintiff's lawyer on the other hand judges success by making recovery for his client. Faced with an initial client application form that may now be outdated and contain some lukewarm financial information and hazy objectives, the lawyer may be encouraged to take the plaintiff's case a step further.

Let me give you an example of a "success" from my client's

49

perspective. The plaintiff's lawyer had made a demand for recovery of losses on a rather speculative stock purchased by a retired plumber through my broker-client. When he sent the demand letter, the plaintiff's lawyer referred to a copy of the initial client account form, several years old, indicating little investment knowledge, and long term growth and income objectives. The plaintiff was on a fixed income. Before I had spoken with the broker, things looked a little dicey.

In responding to any demand, I try to nip the case in the bud immediately. I reply with a very comprehensive letter addressing how the broker satisfied all his obligations, was not negligent and discharged his fiduciary duty if there was one. I attempt to include all facts that demonstrate how the broker has not been remiss. There is no point in holding back information that will come out in discovery or trial. While surprise tactics make dramatic television, we want the matter to end sooner not later. The hope is that when the plaintiff's lawyer discusses the points with his client, he will see there is no merit in proceeding and the matter will end there. To do this I go through the file in detail with the broker, and obtain a complete understanding of the broker's relationship with his client and how he addressed his duties.

In this particular case the new client application form had been filled out by another broker with whom the client had first dealt. A couple of years later the current broker had inherited the client. Over time their relationship had expanded, with almost daily phone calls. Indeed, the client had purchased venture stock on several occasions, some of which was the subject of his claim.

In reviewing the file I came across a piece of paper the other lawyer had conveniently not mentioned (his client hadn't either, I expect). On file, attached to a letter showing that a copy had been mailed to the client some time previously, was a new, updated client application form that the current broker had filled out. Best yet was some of the information scribbled in various places. Client investment knowledge had been upgraded to "good" with a comment that the client (Mr. Smith for our purposes) was a "quick study, had taken time to read several books on the market." Investment objectives had changed to include 25% venture, with a note, "Mr. Smith indicates would like to trade more actively - interested in VSE pennies. Understands risk - said is prepared to lose up to $20,000."

I sent a copy of the updated client application form along with my letter outlining the history of the current broker's relationship with the client to the client's lawyer. That was the last we heard of the matter. In passing, I asked the broker how long it had taken him to fill out the new form. He said he was in the habit of keeping a few blanks on his desk and just filled it in while talking on the phone to Mr. Smith one day. He then had a secretary send it out with a one-line "enclosed herewith please find . . . " letter. The exercise had taken all of a couple of minutes and saved literally thousands of dollars in costs, let alone aggravation!

If you gather from this that I am paying more attention to evidence that you know your client than whether you in fact do, you are partly right. I am not taking away from the importance of knowing your client, but most brokers know their client better than the evidence indicates. Furthermore, you cannot create evidence that you know your client if you don't - so the exercise of itself will ensure compliance. Create the evidence!

Fill out the new account application form, not just completely but with everything you know. Expand on points. And update them - minimum yearly, and with every change in circumstance. For example, there should be an update when your client retires, changes roles, expands his family. And do not get complacent, thinking your "good" clients will never complain. It is equally important to update their file. As in the previous example, a one-line self-serving letter with "enclosed is your updated application form with the new information we discussed" is a tremendously useful piece of evidence.

The object of the exercise is not to create a fictitious paper trail. It is simply to create hard and fast evidence of how well in fact you know your client as you deal with him. That evidence is not generally forthcoming if your client turns into a plaintiff!

Suitability

There would be little point in an obligation to "know your client" if there was no purpose in so doing. It might be argued that the origins of the rule focused on making sure the broker was not conducting business with uncreditworthy

52

clients, but that view is rather cynical. Whatever the origins, it is clearly established that the need to know your client is necessary to fulfil another obligation, or "ought to," which is to review suitability of any trading.

The obligation to review suitability is set out in several places. Provincial regulations exist which direct that dealers make enquiries which are appropriate in order to determine the general investment needs and objective of that client, and the suitability of a proposed purchase or sale for that client.

The IDA regulations use slightly different language, yet to the same effect, stating at regulation 1300.1:

> "Each Member shall use due diligence:
>
> (a)   to learn the essential facts relative to every customer and to every order or account accepted;
>
> (b)   to ensure that the acceptance of any order for any account is within the bounds of good business practice; and
>
> (c)   to ensure that recommendations made for any account are appropriate for the client and in keeping with his investment objectives."

Whatever the source, the regulations and policy simply

incorporate a duty, now accepted by the courts, that a broker and his employer have a duty to consider suitability.

Suitability of an investment is one of the main reasons for knowing your client and if you fail to consider the suitability you have neglected a major "ought to" that puts you at risk if something goes wrong.

Suitability must not only be reviewed within the bounds of the client's objectives, which is within the "mix" of long term, short term, income, venture, mutual fund boxes ticked off in the application form, but also within the standard of good business practice. A highly speculative situation may fail to meet the latter requirement even if it falls within the "mix" in certain situations.

A Suitable Hypothetical

One hypothetical frequently presented at my seminars involves an unsolicited order from a client of little means. In the typical scenario, he wants to place an order which will risk his meagre savings on a venture stock of which the broker knows little. The facts usually involve advising the caller of the lack of information and the risk involved. The broker wants to know if he should take the order.

In these discussions, I work the group through the checklist. In placing the order, will the broker do what he ought to by contract? Yes, assuming he fills the order in keeping with standard practice and that nothing additional was contracted. Going to the other end of the spectrum, is he in a position of a fiduciary? Is there any evidence of reposing trust and reliance on the broker? In the limited facts of the hypothetical, the answer is no. What then of the other duties, the "ought to's" to avoid negligence? If he has asked the questions that allow him to fill out the initial client application form conscientiously, we will assume, for the discussion, that he knows his client as well as can be expected at that point. He knows his client's net worth and that he is risking all his savings. He also knows the client's objectives. Simply put, the client wants this speculative trade. The broker has advised him he knows nothing of the company and that it may be very risky. He has not been negligent in conveying such information as he has, and he was not asked to find out anything more. Does he take the order?

It is interesting to see the varying responses but there is one factor that is troublesome. Often the brokers are inclined to say "yes" based on some extraneous consideration. After all, they reason, the broker seems to be taking care of all the "ought to's." Some brokers are cautious, but try to build on the hypothetical with considerations of whether it was just a one-shot client (in which case they would be disinclined to take the risk). Still others observe that the client could go elsewhere if they didn't take the order, so they may as well. With respect, those considerations would have no bearing on liability.

What is interesting is the response of the managers or supervisors. When I turn to them and ask them if, in their view, taking such an order would be in keeping with good business practice, almost universally their answer is negative.

The exercise illustrates a potential problem. If the industry's own experts, the people with knowledge and experience and with the duty to supervise, concur it would be outside the realm of good business practice to take the order, who can defend the broker who does? If a proposed situation causes debate, it is not necessarily cause for rejection. But make a careful examination of your role in light of the reasonable broker, and consider good business practice. Do not restrict your consideration to what you think; take into account your fellow professionals' view. Consider what your compliance officer or manager will say. If in doubt, ask him or her for their assessment. If it goes to court, you can bet the plaintiff's lawyer will ask someone like them.

Fitting the "mix"

There remains the question of reviewing whether a particular purchase fits within a client's objectives. If the account application form indicates 75% long-term and the client is considering a Vancouver Stock Exchange venture stock, make a quick tally to see how much he could invest in that category. This is especially important if he has picked up a few flyers along the way. If his account has a net worth of $40,000, most of which is in long term blue chips, but has $3,000 to $4,000 scattered among a few juniors, putting another $10,000 in a venture situation can cause problems if there is no clear evidence of a change in his objectives.

Sure I'll take your order for $500 of Consolidated Moose Pasture. Just let me fill out this New Account Application Form. What did you say the address of the men's shelter was?

If he still wants the stock he needs to be told that the trade indicates a change in his objectives, that is, in the "mix" he has indicated. Examine the suitability in light of his financial position and objectives. At the very least a revised application form showing the increase in venture exposure is warranted. As in my earlier example, filling out a new form while you are talking to your client on the phone, noting the discussion and his desire to increase the risk, then mailing it to him with a simple cover letter, a copy of which you keep, will go a long way to preventing problems.

Classifying the Investment

There is a second responsibility that gives brokers concern and that is classifying the investment. Certain investments are easier to categorize. Government bonds, preferred shares with dividend coverage may readily fit within a consensus view. A mutual fund is generally recognized as such (although care should be taken to note that many have unique features).

On the other hand, classification of high risk venture situations is also generally not difficult. Most brokers understand that small companies on junior exchanges fall within the venture (speculative) category.

Difficulty more frequently arises in stocks where classification is less clear. We all know of stocks that at one time were considered long-term growth that have proven to be disastrous. Then too there have been small companies that have done nothing but make consistent, solid advances.

How should a broker assess those? Can a broker achieve some comfort without having to take steps that interfere with his production?

The task is not so onerous when we consider that his duty in this regard, his "ought to," is to behave as the reasonable man, more specifically the reasonable broker.

It is by that standard of conduct that the broker will be judged in reviewing his allocation of investment to different categories. Specifically he will not have to live up to the standard of an investment analyst for example, nor will he be construed as a guarantor of performance. The test is whether, exercising the skill attributable to his profession, the broker acted reasonably in categorizing the investment as he did.

I realize that to some degree we are answering the question with another question, but there are some factors to consider that will help.

First, it would be difficult to argue with the reasonableness of relying on a firm's research conclusions. In some provinces securities commission's policies go so far as to specify that a broker's recommendation should be based on his firm's research. Research departments are set up to provide that kind of advice. If the broker is not aware of any reason why he should not rely on such information, it is doubtful that he would be found to have acted unreasonably in concurring with the research department's categorization of an investment.

(As an aside, the conclusions by the research analyst will face a different test - was it reasonable for the analyst, exercising skill commensurate with his position, to make such a conclusion? If not, the analyst, and the firm that put out his recommendation may be negligent, but not likely the broker who in good faith relied on the conclusion.)

As the broker moves away from professional analysis and relies more on his own resources, he is increasing the likelihood of challenge to his conclusions. That is not to say that he is acting unreasonably, but he must have clear and reasonable grounds for his conclusions.

There are, of course, stocks with well-proven track records and broadly disseminated information that will be subject of little debate. But as consensus reduces, risk increases.

In my seminars I frequently illustrate the problem by throwing out the names of some stocks of well-known mid-size companies that have not been subject to a firm's analysis. Immediately there is a debate among brokers, with some members putting the stock in any one of three categories, each having cogent reasons for doing so. For good measure, when there is more than one analyst present they will often disagree among themselves.

That is not to say a broker can only deal with stocks that have his firm's recommendation or categorization. Relying on verifiable information and passing that on is not unreasonable conduct, but it does not exonerate the duty to make sure that the investment is within the client's objectives. Risk arises when the broker takes on too much of the role of analyst and tries to make conclusions in that capacity. If he starts taking on the role of analyst he is going to be judged by the standards applicable to that profession. The last thing a broker needs is a new set of standards and a longer list of "ought to's."

The solution when dealing with stocks that do not have firm analysis and recommendation, or at the very least uncontroversial recognition - and by that I mean no one would argue with the reasonableness of the assumption - is not to jump to your own conclusion as to the conservativeness of the investment for the purpose of making it fit within your client's indicated objectives. If something goes wrong you will find the reasonableness of your conclusions under attack. You don't want to be sitting in a courtroom watching lawyers play the grown-up version of "my daddy is smarter than your daddy," i.e., my expert is better than your expert.

If the plaintiff produces one credible expert who can argue that your conclusion was wrong, you have a problem. Remember, the judge will have heard from the hapless client who of course was relying on your expertise. Next, the judge will have seen that your expert witness' conclusion differs from that of the equally credible plaintiff's expert. While hindsight should not have a bearing in deciding which expert to give credence to, the judge will be confronted with the fact that the plaintiff's expert conclusions might have been the better one, since the stock did go down. (If it hadn't, the plaintiff wouldn't be there, would he? I have yet to see someone argue suitability on even the most outrageous flyer when it goes up.)

The safer approach is simply to assume that the investment falls within a riskier category and ensure that there is room for that within the client's stated objective mix. If you know your client and you know the investment is commensurate with his objectives and there are reasons why the stock is a fit, make sure his client application reflects that. He is not likely to take objection to an updated client application form that reflects revised objectives if he wants the trade.

Other Duties

In our consideration of negligence - a review of the ought to's that a reasonable broker would do - we have focused on knowing your client and reviewing suitability. Those are the most readily identifiable areas of concern but not the only obligations.

Again, it is not practical to try and come up with an exhaustive list. No matter how we tried we could not cover every point and we would begin an exercise that would begin to encroach on our principal focus, that of providing a level of comfort without being counterproductive.

The more effective approach is to consider, in reviewing your conduct with your client, whether you have done all the things a reasonable broker would do. As a professional, you should be able to make a good assessment of your conduct if you are considering the matter intelligently and without

Of course the stocks were long-term growth, your Honour. It will be years before they will be worth what the client paid for them.

bias. You also have access to other resources to assist you - your registered representative manuals, and in-house guidelines. Remember, when you are conducting yourself within your industry guidelines, you have gone a long way toward fulfilling your obligation to act as the reasonable broker.

There will, of course, always be debatable issues. One that frequently arises is the question concerning ongoing contact and dissemination of information to the client. A common question is whether a broker, having had a client buy a stock on his recommendation or with his consultation, has an obligation to pass on new information and keep him apprised of developments of the particular company.

I do not have a specific conclusion but can offer some considerations for guidance. Reporting issuers - those companies who can distribute securities to the public - have extensive reporting requirements including obligations to issue press releases on material developments. They are subject to further regulations dealing with continuous disclosure to shareholders. Assuming that this information is reaching the client, either through his registration on shareholder lists or diligently passed on by the firm, he should be well informed. On the other hand, if the investment was recommended because of information only the broker had, the client might assume he would be apprised of developments in that regard. I have not yet been able to obtain a consensus view, and the industry practice seems mixed. And, as we will see under the next heading, there is a great likelihood that it may be a duty if there is a fiduciary relationship with the client. Responsibility for ongoing communication does not seem clear. It may behoove the industry to adopt clear guidelines before we have the courts deciding what the reasonable broker ought to do in the situation.

Fiduciary Relationships

In determining whether you have fulfilled your obligations in a fiduciary relationship, it goes without saying that the first step is to establish whether you have such a relationship with your client.

Frankly, asking yourself if a fiduciary relationship exists with each client is a worthwhile exercise. As pointed out earlier, arguing there is a fiduciary relationship is a powerful plaintiff's tool that is becoming increasingly popular in pleadings.

Am I a Fiduciary?

Certainly not every broker-client relationship contains fiduciary responsibility. It is in each case a question of fact. Again, trying to prepare a list of examples would not assure that every potential situation would be included.

The better approach is to bear in mind the key elements that lead the courts to conclude when such a relationship exists.

In *Rhoads* we have seen the court summarize a number of

cases to develop one test, that being a relationship where one person is vulnerable to another and is liable to be hurt if the first person breaches the trust reposed in him.

When your client is relying on you, and placing trust in you and you accept that trust, he is vulnerable to your failure to exercise that trust.   That is the essence of a fiduciary relationship.

Examine your relationship.   Ask yourself if your client is trusting you on some point, relying on you for something more than making suggestions for him to consider and filling his orders once he has made up his mind.

Consider your client's reliance on you in light of your knowledge of the client's sophistication.   The less knowledgeable he is, the more likely the argument that he has placed reliance on your advice and judgement.

As a corollary, examine why this person is using you instead of someone else. Now consider what you think would be your client's answer to that question. What would he tell his lawyer was the reason he was using you? Would he argue that he had entrusted you with some control over his affairs or at the decisions he made?

Consider this: could the client use any other broker in your office in the normal course? If you went away on vacation would you have to give the broker covering your absence any particular instructions as to what this client might expect or how he is to be handled?

Ask yourself if there is something particular your client expects you to do, and whether he will be hurt if you don't take care of that particular responsibility. A general request from a client that you call him with good ideas from time to time is not likely to result in vulnerability. A directive to acquire preferred shares from companies that have sufficient earnings to cover dividends leaves him vulnerable if you don't carry out that instruction.

A red flag should go up when dealing with clients who have told you that they don't know anything about the market, or don't understand anything about stocks - and that they are relying solely on your judgement. Such situations are fraught with hazards and almost certainly will be considered fiduciary if you accept the responsibility.

Be honest in your assessment. If your client is relying on you for something outside the normal broker-client relationship, consider the possibility that a fiduciary relationship exists. The plaintiff's lawyer almost certainly will.

Fiduciary "Ought To's"

If you have concluded that you have a fiduciary relationship, then there exists an expanded list of obligations or more "ought to's."

Those additional obligations consist of a responsibility to advise the client carefully, fully, honestly and in good faith and to carry out the client's intention. In doing so, the broker must exercise skill and diligence appropriate to the situation.

The obligations at first glance may seem at once very broad, and yet vague. Very few brokers would admit to being less than careful and honest when trying to carry out their client's wishes. A broker almost always feels he has demonstrated good faith and exercised appropriate skill and diligence.

The real challenge in a fiduciary relationship is to focus on the extra elements that go beyond the usual broker-client responsibility - those that created the fiduciary relationship in the first place. The expectation that created the vulnerability is the obligation that needs to be fulfilled, which is the extra "ought to" in the relationship.

On that point, on the nexus of vulnerability and duty, it is worth looking at *Rhoads* again. The Rhoads wanted income. They made it plain that was their objective and that they were relying on the Yzenbrandts to find investments that met that objective, yet they were sold equity mutual funds. In a non-fiduciary relationship the Yzenbrandts might have argued successfully that in the final analysis, the Rhoads had made the decision. They had been given mutual fund prospectuses. But the basis of finding the fiduciary relationship had been the Rhoads' "little or no" investment knowledge and the placing of their trust and reliance on the Yzenbrandts to fulfil their wishes, in particular with regard to income investments. It was that related failing - the trust that the Yzenbrandts would find income investments, and their not doing so - that created liability.

The second breach of fiduciary duty occurred when the Yzenbrandts failed to warn the Rhoads of the "scary" market conditions. Again, the court points out that this duty arose by the nature of the relationship with the Rhoads - the Yzenbrandts were aware that the Rhoads did not want to take risks, and had promised that the Rhoads would be warned if there were any problems. Mrs. Yzenbrandt admitted that she was aware of her husband's letter recommending that investors get out of equity markets.

The Rhoads were vulnerable, having put their trust in the Yzenbrandts to take care of certain matters, in this case, advising them of problems in the market. The Yzenbrandts had accepted that particular responsibility and then failed to discharge the duty that had been entrusted to them.

The obligations that you must discharge in a fiduciary relationship are not an endless catalogue of responsibilities, but are those relating to the specific trust reposed in you by your client. The courts have made it clear that both sides must be considered in their interaction.

When a fiduciary duty exists it must be discharged with care, skill and diligence. There is to be no compromise on that. If you have an obligation resulting from a fiduciary relationship your performance will be judged by the highest standards applicable to your profession. That is not to say there is not a reasonableness test. In *Rhoads* the court found that the Yzenbrandts had not made reasonable efforts to contact the Rhoads when they were on holiday. The court had not imposed an absolute obligation. The failure occurred when the Yzenbrandts had done nothing but mail the letter to the Rhoads' home address knowing they were on vacation, after having been given a number by which the Rhoads could have been contacted.

There is an important distinction in the application of reasonableness in a fiduciary relationship. In the absence of a fiduciary relationship, the question of whether a broker is negligent for failing to do something may be considered in the light of whether that "something" is an action a reasonable broker would do in the circumstances. An obligation arising out of a fiduciary situation does not have to pass that test - there is an absolute obligation to do it. The question of reasonableness then goes to the quality of the performance of the task. Given that the broker will be held to all the skill, care and diligence of his profession, reasonableness only comes into issue as to the satisfactory performance of the task, not in considering whether it should have been done.

While it is impossible to come up with a list of fiduciary obligations, two areas are often of concern.

One concern is communication. We have seen an example of the problem in *Rhoads*. The failure to communicate information is a common pleading in fiduciary relationships. Again reasonableness will be considered, but only in the context of the sufficiency of performance, if the duty exists.

Hence, a broker cannot be faulted for failing to anticipate, seer-like, that a company will be suspending its dividend payments if there has been no previous indication. However, failing to pass on announcements of material adverse changes in a timely fashion can create problems where the client, with your acceptance, has reposed that trust in you.

Another problematic relationship is one where the client argues "I didn't know anything about the market, I was just relying on my broker." If the client can make that stick as the basis of the relationship, it almost certainly is fiduciary, with a broad field of obligations.

In fact, the first thing to consider in such a situation is whether you want that client, or if you want to put him in anything but the most conservative investments. Certainly consideration should be given to turning his account over to an investment advisor or portfolio manager.

The fact is however, that while many clients may express such a sentiment, and will certainly argue that it was the basis of the relationship to their lawyers when considering a lawsuit, in truth it is not often an accurate expression of their situation. It remains for the broker to make sure, before dealing with the account, that the relationship is better defined.

For that we go back to some basic "ought to's" starting with "know your client." Someone unsophisticated in the market may still want long term growth investments, or mutual funds that have capital appreciation or income potential. If such an objective is established, it is not beyond the purview of a broker to carefully explain the risks and make recommendations that fit within those parameters. Even if a fiduciary relationship exists, the broker can still discharge his duties, notwithstanding depreciation of the investment.

Just because the client has reposed trust in the broker to do certain things (for example purchase long term growth securities) the broker will not be liable for losses if he has made recommendations, exercising due care and skill, and some unforseen event occurs. The risk in fiduciary obligations is not so much that the broker cannot perform his obligations, but, because he does not appreciate what they are, he fails to carry them out. Listen to what your client expects of you, make sure both you and he are of a same mind as to what he is entrusting you to do and the responsibility you have accepted. Once you are clear as to what your duty is, discharge it carefully, fully, honestly with skill and diligence.

Do not accept responsibilities you cannot discharge. In one seminar I was quizzed on a situation concerning an unsophisticated client telling his broker to buy stocks that "would go up." In a diligent attempt to know his client, the broker inquired "and what if they don't go up?"

The client, obviously a Will Rogers fan, replied, "Then don't buy them."

My advice? Send him to a competitor.

THE CHECKLIST

Duties vary as the relationship changes. It is necessary to be able to quickly analyze the relationship to understand the scope of duties. Focusing on one aspect may lead to dangerous omissions. A brief, disciplined approach through a series of questions, will avoid missing issues.

What I have observed during the many hypothetical cases raised in the question and answer period following my seminars is that a constant source of frustration to brokers is understanding the relationship they have with their client, and ascertaining the corresponding duties.

In point of fact, more often than not the question was focused on the obligation - the "What should I do in this situation?" This is somewhat like putting the cart before the horse. First understand the nature of your relationship, and then go through the list of attendant responsibilities to see if you have fulfilled them. And equally important, make sure there is evidence that you have.

This guide has pointed out several times that it is not possible to give a comprehensive list of all obligations. Broker-client relationships are just too complex to catalogue all possibilities, and given the number of, shall we say "ingenious" situations brokers have presented, I would not begin to try.

73

But what I can do is provide a series of questions, which, like a series of filters, defines certain duties to consider at each level.

Call it linear logic, or "thinking like a lawyer," or, for convenience, a "checklist" if you wish, but it is really a thought process for helping determining what your obligations are. In the final analysis, we are still trying to establish the "ought to's."

If you have a specific question as to what you should do in a particular situation, or even a general concern about your overall responsibility to a client, it will be helpful to analyze the situation in the following steps, in each case, from beginning to end. The exercise only takes a few moments, and will help you readily identify problematic areas.

The Checklist

Contract

• Have all the terms in the written contracts - account agreements, margin accounts etc. - been taken care of?

• Have all implied terms been taken care of - have actions been carried out in accordance with stock exchange rules and sound industry practice?

• Has there been a promise to do something more, something that could be construed as a term of contract? Has there been an undertaking to do something that, if it hadn't been promised, meant this client would not be dealing with you? If so, is it taken care of?

Negligence

Know Your Client

- Is the new client application form filled out - completely? Does it include additional information known about the client?

- Is the client application form updated to reflect the trading currently being done? Is it more than a year old?

- Does the client application form or other correspondence provide evidence of how well the client is known, of the risks he is prepared to take, of discussions with him?

- Is there evidence that any particular facts are known - e.g., limits on income, current financial situation?

Suitability

- Does the account form accurately reflect the client's objectives mix? Should it be updated?

- Are the recommendations clearly, indisputably,

within the objectives - is there a strong basis for categorizing each investment - i.e., firm recommendation or total consensus?

- If any stocks are questionable - if they were found to be "riskier" - would they still fit within the client's objectives? Does the client account form or other evidence indicate that the client knowingly accepted this level of risk?

- Does the total dollar value of each category of investment fit within the client's "mix" of objectives?

- Does the file clearly provide evidence of suitability of each type of investment?

Other

- Is the account being handled as a reasonable broker would?

- Are the account activities in keeping with good business practice?

- Is the client's account handled within industry standards, regulations and in-house guidelines?

- Is there something not being taken care of that could result in loss? Would a reasonable broker take care of this?

Fiduciary Relationship

- Is there a fiduciary relationship - has the client trusted you to do something, which you have agreed to, which if not done, leaves him vulnerable?

- Have you taken care of that extra something, carefully, fully, honestly and in good faith and exercised professional skill and diligence in carrying out the client's intention?

- Does the client file, through new and updated client application forms, correspondence, notes and memos provide evidence of all of the foregoing?

SOME SUGGESTIONS

Two categories of suggestions - ones that can be implemented by the broker almost immediately, and others that require co-operation - reduce risk and improve client relations without interfering with production. The list is not exhaustive and can be varied and improved. They are ideas that show what can be done.

The thrust of this guide has been to give practical, not theoretical, advice. The objective is to reduce risk without interfering with production.

To achieve that objective, we have examined the origins and component elements that give rise to broker liability - breach of contract, negligence and breach of fiduciary duty. We have reduced complex legal theory to the concept of "ought to" - and recognized that as broker-client relationships vary, so do the obligations, the "ought to's." We have focused on how obligations arise to provide a methodology for thinking, rather than try to create a list of duties.

Notwithstanding an aversion to lists, in a section entitled "The Checklist" we have provided some steps as guidance to reviewing a situation. The purpose is to allow for a quick, functional analysis to quickly focus on areas of concern. Combined with an understanding of the legal foundation for those concerns, the broker can hopefully find some fast, practical solutions.

Some Limitations

The following suggestions are presented not as an exhaustive list, but rather to assist in thinking. The suggestions, along with the remarks as to their utility and consequences, are meant to give the broker ideas as to how even simple things can significantly assist in reducing risk. Some ideas may appeal immediately, in the form suggested. Others, it may be argued, are impractical in their suggested form by virtue of the office the broker works in, the assistance he has, or the nature of the way the broker practices. That need not diminish the utility of examining the idea. Variations on the theme are allowable, and no doubt better solutions are possible. But if the germ of the idea is planted, I will have achieved my goal, regardless of the specific form of the solution that takes root. And I have little doubt members of the industry will come up with a host of variations and suggestions not mentioned here. I look forward to hearing about them.

Some Ideas

Here then are some suggestions:

- Complete an "expanded" new account application form every time you open an account. This is so important, and yet so simple. It will be the first thing a client's lawyer will want to see, and the best tool for turning away a potential claim. Frankly, I'd redesign the thing with boxes for a lot more detail, or at the very least, duplicate it at twice the existing

No, Mr. Investigator, my broker did not make recommendations in keeping with my investment objectives. I told him I wanted stocks that would go up!

size, *and then fill it out with additional information.*
Even in its present form, write on the back, attach
additional sheets. Find out about your client and
then prove it! You can turn questioning your client
about his affairs from a formality into an ingratiating
experience. Who doesn't want to talk about
themselves? You can fill in the details while talking
to him, while on the phone, immediately after the
fact. But get the information on the form, and give
him a copy. All of this takes minutes.

- Update the client account form, at the very least
annually, and especially if you are taking over an
existing client from another broker, or you are
executing a trade for a client that has been inactive.
Things change. Client's incomes, needs and
objectives change. The next worst thing after an
incomplete form is a dated one. The plaintiff's
lawyer will make mincemeat of an old form that
doesn't reflect current reality, or one filled out by a
previous broker. So, by the way, will the IDA. Keep
a stack of blanks on your desk.

- Update client account forms when the client changes
some aspect of his trading. The client who has
$50,000 in long-term growth will instruct his lawyer
to take the case to the discovery stage if he has even
$2,000 in a venture situation that's not reflected on
his form!

- In all update situations, send the client the new form

immediately. Getting him to acknowledge by signature is great, but failing that, even a one-line cover letter "enclosed herewith your updated form ..." is strong evidence.

- Here's a great way to finesse updated account forms - have a standard form of covering letter go out, signed by your office manager or supervisor. This can work as a great marketing tool. Think of the effect a letter would have, signed by such officer, to the effect ... "herewith your updated form. We have reviewed your situation and objectives with your account executive ... as always, if you have any questions, please feel free to call him, or the undersigned (manager)." You can add language about your additional services, facilities etc. The client is going to feel good about the extra attention, not be put off by the amended form. And you can create a general letter that can go out with everyone's updated form. It will still only take moments to have the standard letter run off, reviewed and signed. Then you will have proof of two people taking care of their duties - the broker and his manager.

- Create and use a standard letter when objectives change to include "riskier" investments. Rather than intimidate a client, this too can foster good will. A warning dealing with the scope of the risk can be coupled with a discussion of the firm's facilities and resources. But you are creating evidence that risk was discussed, and if the client is going to complain, it should have at the time, not later. We are still talking minuscule amounts of time here!

- Do memos to file on important conversations, meetings with clients, phone calls. This does not have to be onerous - the memos need neither be formal nor typed. A memo pad with blanks for dates and names will do, or even blank sheets. Jotting down salient points about conversations on risk, objectives or developments can be important evidence. Memos made during conversations and put on file are producible evidence.

- Keep a business day timer. I don't necessarily mean a diary - just a log of appointments, significant calls, meetings. Keep the timer open on your desk for easy use, and keep them from year to year. They can prove invaluable evidence of ongoing relations. You would be surprised how often frequent client contact can turn into "he'd call me once in a while" at discovery. Current entries in a diary are producible evidence. Use the day timer for business entries. Short notations as to time, place and topic will be a big help eg., "August 29 ... phoned Mr. Smith at office re: risk on XYZ Capital."

- Make sure you keep a running tally of the dollar value in the "mix" of your clients investments. It seems obvious, but you would not believe the number of times the broker has been surprised to find that a client's portfolio is 50% venture when his account form limits that to 10%. It happens easily, especially if the value of the other investments drop, you could be dead in the water. If the dollar value is outside of the mix, discuss selling the offending investment - and then if the client wants to keep the stock - send him an updated form and covering letter! At least from that time forward he wouldn't be able to complain. He was under an obligation to mitigate damages if he didn't want the stock at that time.

- In appropriate situations, have another member attend with you at client meetings. Again, this doesn't need to be intimidating. Introducing a fellow broker who "has additional experience" or a sales assistant who can help, can give positive vibes yet provide valuable confirmation on important discussions concerning risk, changed objectives, etc.

- Document sources of recommendations. If they are the subject of a firm's research, keep your own copy of the findings, memos etc. Ideally, copy the information to the client. Again, the quick "enclosed herewith" letter (copy kept on file) is a time-efficient way of providing evidence. Where recommendations are from other sources, keep records. If there is nothing to send the client, more effort is required. Notes on conversations explaining source of information and the extent of qualification, or limitation, on the information is good, but not as good as a confirming letter. There is no question that feedback from your analyst will go a long way to establishing the reasonableness of any judgment call you had to make on suitability.

- Where the nature of an investment could be subject to controversy, assume it falls in the "riskier" category. Then review the client's stated objective mix against his portfolio. If the dollar value doesn't fit, consider whether his account forms should reflect a change in objective. If, on discussion with the client, it appears his objectives have been altered to include the stock in his mix, update the account form, and send him a confirming copy.

- Develop several "standard form" covering letters to be used by yourself, or ideally, your manager, to facilitate evidence of communication with your client. The previous suggestions are examples of when their use is valuable - updating accounts, changes of objectives, passing on information. Other situations too may arise. The value is two-fold.

Firstly, some thought can be given to creating good covering letters without immediate time constraints. When their use is warranted, they should be sent out immediately, so that damages, if any, can be mitigated. A little planning, even a collaborative effort, can, and in the past, has produced some excellent letters. They not only communicated the information necessary to reduce risk, but enhanced client comfort and relations.

Secondly, there is nothing like inertia to stop a good idea. The middle of a busy day is not the time for a broker to devote energy to creating a well-balanced communication. Frankly, brokers, like most professionals, will balk at taking a break from their income-producing activities to do something that will require extra effort. Balancing the immediate desire to do something productive against an expenditure of time on something that may not become a problem will result in delay. The delay further lessens the likelihood of getting it done, until the necessity has passed or it is too late.

Having the forms of letters prepared in advance relieves the broker from having to spend time dreaming up a letter each time communication is warranted, can provide excellent public relations, and with a minimum outlay of time, provides strong evidence that can discourage unwarranted claims.

- When reviewing a client relationship, either generally or with respect to a particular matter, examine all the aspects of the relationship, not just isolated points. Discipline your thinking to use an approach like that in the Checklist, so that nothing is missed. Remember that in any broker liability case, failure to cover off any one of the areas of obligation is enough to incur liability. *Rhoads* had the three - contract, negligence and fiduciary duties. But as the Court of

Appeal demonstrated, any one was enough to uphold the decision that the brokers were responsible for loss.

Some Other Suggestions and Observations

While the foregoing ideas include some suggestions that can be readily implemented, even by a broker working alone, there are some other suggestions, which, while taking more effort to implement, can assist in the objective of providing efficient methods of reducing risk. They will, however, entail collaboration among managers, brokers, administrators, their professional advisors and, in some cases, joint effort among member firms in the industry. These areas include:

•   Revision to account application forms and update procedures. My concerns with the lack of information on the prescribed new client application form has already been discussed. However, since many jurisdictions recognize IDA approved forms for regulation purposes, effort should also be concentrated on a new form, recognized by that body and the stock exchanges.

   The desired result should be a form that, when completed, will meet any challenge concerning a broker being cognizant of all salient information concerning his client, especially in light of recent court decisions.

Updating procedures should be regularized. While almost all firms boast of a procedure, most brokers are unaware of its existence, and there is little evidence of habitual practice. As discussed, once implemented the practice should involve minimal time and yet produce a very high level of dissuasion against unwarranted claims.

- Contracts should be revised, to the extent possible, to clarify obligations and exclude extraneous undertakings. The sum of the written agreements for brokers' services, account operating forms and the like, can be improved significantly. There are indeed limits to which liability can be excluded by contract, and courts tend to construe exculpatory clauses narrowly and work around them where possible. Consideration too must be given to client response to obvious attempts to limit acceptable responsibility. The problems do not reduce the usefulness of the exercise. Even if the desired level of legal obligation cannot be totally curtailed (and it likely cannot), it will help by raising the issue and perhaps avoid misunderstandings by both client and broker alike. With professional input, there is room for significant improvement in these documents.

- There should be a consistent approach to responses to regulatory investigations of complaints, both to the stock exchange and IDA. I am not suggesting for a moment anything less than candid co-operation nor necessarily legal representation at early stages. But my experience indicates approach varies widely, from brokers responding totally unassisted to needlessly formal replies. There are several concerns.

Firstly, a potential plaintiff receives, at virtually no cost, the benefit of a negative finding. While an IDA ruling does not of itself give rise necessarily to civil liability, a finding of breach of professional conduct goes a long way to supporting a case of negligence. While the broker may be prepared to accept disciplinary rulings, fines, rewrites, supervision and the like, resultant civil liability may be far more serious. An unprepared broker, particularly one who has not gone through the process before, may unwittingly focus on a certain aspect of his conduct that he feels exonerates him, only to find that he has hung himself on another point. More than once I have seen negative outcomes based on the broker's own statements, sometimes made peripherally to the matter under investigation. It can be helpful to have a manager or supervisor present during interviews, if not a lawyer. Much more satisfying results are achieved when the broker understands the implications of all the issues and can explain and demonstrate all salient matters relating to his conduct.

It must be remembered that when a broker responds to a complaint, the investigator has already heard the client's side of the story. The investigator has larger resources at his disposal, and the story told to him by a client who has suffered loss generally, in keeping with human nature, contains only the complainant's version of the evidence. I am not suggesting in the least that investigators are biased - in point of fact my observations are that they take pains to be fair and balanced in their approach.   But, notwithstanding any informality, the interests of the complainant are adverse, and it behooves the broker and the industry to make sure that their side is clearly and fully set forth.

•   Similarly there should be consistency in the approach to broker liability suits. Counsel with experience and knowledge in the industry should be used. For much the same reason as the insurers of medical malpractice retain a handful of counsel, the industry needs representatives conversant with the business, its jargon and practice. This is particularly true with a developing area such as broker liability. One of the roles of counsel is to make sure the judge is aware both of practice and law relating to the issues. Even experienced litigators and seasoned judges may be short on experience with the issues pertaining to broker liability if it was not an area familiar to their practice. The lawyer needs to be familiar with the business, know what questions to ask and what usual and acceptable practice is. He may have to "educate" the judge through the evidence presented. Some of the poorer decisions clearly reflect a lack of understanding, leaving the case reports littered with inconsistent and damaging precedents.

- To the extent the industry can, it should clarify by policy and procedure areas where practice is inconsistent or repeatedly the subject of litigation. One area discussed in the previous text is the broker's responsibility for ongoing communication concerning developments by a corporation in which the client has invested. Responsibilities with respect to unsolicited orders, and distinction between the obligations of full-service brokers versus discount brokers are areas that need to be addressed. If the industry does not establish guidelines the courts will.

- Ongoing education, with emphasis on the solution, not the problem, is needed. Fears of unwarranted concerns can be allayed by focusing on understanding and a methodology for reducing risk. In-house meetings, bulletins and seminars can be brief, yet effective means for providing the broker with the tools to reduce risk in his practice.

The latter suggestions obviously require concerted effort and not insignificant work. The important result, however, is that while the implementation will require an outlay of time by the industry, the remedies will not interfere with production. At the end of the day the broker will be less encumbered with concerns over potential liability and enjoy more freedom to boldly carry out his profession.

Also from Mistaya Publishing Ltd.

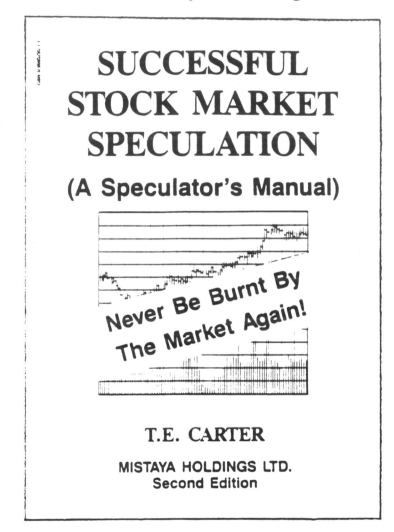

SUCCESSFUL STOCK MARKET SPECULATION

(A Speculator's Manual)

Never Be Burnt By The Market Again!

T.E. CARTER

MISTAYA HOLDINGS LTD.
Second Edition

The best seller by Ted Carter that is a must for anyone wanting to speculate in the market.

To order, mail cheque or money order for $17.95 to Mistaya Publishing Ltd. c/o 1800, 350 - 7th Avenue S.W., Calgary, Alberta, T2P 3N9.